An inside View of the House of Commons.

THE
Infant Lawyer;
or the
GOVERNMENT of ENGLAND.
Explained to the capacity of
Youth.

This is a proper
NEW YEARS GIFT

from a Father who wishes his Son to have a clear
Idea of the GOVERNMENT of the Country in which he
lives, and also from those who intend their Sons for
the Bar, or an Attorney's Office, as the nature of the
several Courts and Inns of Law are particularly
described in the most simple and easy language.

BY A LAWYER.

LONDON:

Printed and Sold by Iohn Marshall,
N°.4, Aldermary Church Yard, Bow Lane,
and N°.17, Queen Street, Cheapside.

THE

INFANT LAWYER, &c.

Of the GOVERNMENT *of* ENGLAND.

ENGLAND is a monarchy, that is governed by one perfon, who is called

A K I N G.

His Title.

By the Grace of God, King of Great Britain, France, and Ireland, *Defender of the Faith.*

Defender of the Faith, although ufed before by the Kings of England

B   was

was confirmed to be their right in consequence of a book written by Henry VIIIth. againſt a man of the name of *Luther*, who oppoſed the catholic religion.

PERSON.

The King of England is crowned, an honor which the kings of Spain, Portugal, and other kings have not. At his coronation he is anointed with oil, a cuſtom which has laſted a thouſand years.

Of the life and ſafety of his perſon the laws of England make it the greateſt of all crimes only to imagine his death, or to kill any of his judges, when performing their duty, is equally as bad, as they are

ſuppoſed

suppofed to reprefent him, and doing his bufinefs.—This crime is called *High Treafon*.

OFFICE.

He promifes at his coronation to protect the clergy, to preferve his own rights, and to do juftice, love mercy, keep peace, &c.

SUPERIORITY.

Allows of none fuperior to himfelf. He is the perfon from whom all juftice is derived. He may, if he choofes, fit in any of the courts, as the Englifh Kings formerly did.

POWER.

The King has certain powers, or more commonly called *privileges*,

B 2   placed

placed in him, in order that he may the better perform the duties of his office. He may himself alone, without the affistance of *Parliament,* (a word that will be explained in it's proper place) *declare war againft other countries, make-peace, fend and receive Ambaffadors,* (people who are fent from one court to another) *make treaties* (that is, agreements) *with foreign kingdoms,* befides many other things.

He may, if he choofes, *adjourn* the Parliament, (that is, put off the fitting for a certain time) or break it up entirely, which is called *diffolving* it. He alone has the appointment of all land and fea officers, the choice of magiftrates and bifhops, people high in the church, and alfo many other privileges.   DOMINIONS.

DOMINIONS.

The dominions of the King of England are *this Country, Scotland,* and *Ireland,* with several other places.

REVENUES.

His revenues mean his yearly profits. They are perhaps greater than any other king in Europe.

THE RESPECT SHEWN TO HIM.

No king has more respect paid him. Those people who present any address or paper to him kneel on one knee. All persons (except the Prince of Wales) stand without their hats before him.

THE

THE CROWN.

By the laws of England the King has a right to the crown, and is immediately succeeded at his death by his son, or next relation, without waiting for the consent of the people.

If the deceased King (that is, the King who dies) has left no sons, then the crown goes to his *eldest daughter*. For want of daughter then to his *brother*, and for want of brother then to his *sister*.

MINORITY.

This means the time before the King grows up to be a man; during which period persons are appointed as his masters to instruct him. These are generally chosen from among the first people in the country.

ABSENCE.

If the King go to any other country, then some person or persons are appointed to act in his place during his absence.

INCAPACITY.

This means when the king is not able or capable, by reason of *disease*, *weakness*, or *old age*, to do his duty. In that case a person is chosen to act for him, and he is called a *Regent*.

THE QUEEN.

The King's Wife. During the life of the King she has as many privileges as any Queen in Europe. She is thought the *second great Person*

in

in the kingdom, and it is one of the
greateſt crimes that can be committed even to think of putting her to
death, and is alſo called *Higb Treaſon.* There is as much reſpect paid
to her as to the King.

OF THE SONS AND DAUGHTERS OF THE KING.

THE ELDEST SON,

From the day of his birth is called
Prince of Wales, a title that was firſt
given by king Edward I. to his eldeſt
ſon. For the Welch nation being
unwilling to ſubmit to ſtrangers, the
King ordered that his Queen ſhould
be delivered of her firſt child in Caer-
narvon caſtle in Wales, and then
aſked the Welch if they would be
content

content to fubjeft themfelves to one of their own nation, to which they confented. The child was then created *Prince of Wales*.

The king's eldeft fon is alfo by right Duke of *Cornwall*, *Earl of Chefter*, and has many other titles.

DIGNITY.

The Prince in our law is reputed as the fame perfon with the King. To imagine his death is made *High Treafon*, and in almoft every cafe is as much refpected as either the King or Queen.

THE YOUNGER SONS.

The King's younger fons are creat-ed *Dukes* or *Earls* of any places he

thinks

thinks proper. They are all as foon
as born confidered *Counfellors of State*,
that is, perfons, when they grow up,
who may be confulted upon bufinefs
that refpect the nation.

To all the King's children belong
the titles of *Royal Highnefs*. In their
prefence all perfons are to appear
without their hats, and kneel whenever they are permitted to kifs their
hands.

The King's daughters are ftiled
Princeffes, the eldeft of whom is called the *Princefs Royal*.

Having now done with the Royal
Family, we fhall begin to treat of that
part of our Government called

ECCLESIASTICAL.

ECCLESIASTICAL.

This means that part which refpects the Religion of the country; and the firft great men that attract our attention are the two *Archbifhops*, or, as they are fometimes called, *Primates.* They are at the head of the Church. One called *Archbifhop of Canterbury*, the other *Archbifhop of York*, two cities in England. They have great power or what we called before, *privileges.* Under them are twenty four

BISHOPS.

Thefe are perfons who rank next to the Archbifhops in confequence. In each city in England there is a church, much larger than our common churches, called a *Cathedral*, to
which

which belongs a *Bishop*, who is considered head of the place, and has the
conducting of every thing there respecting the Church. The greatest
among them is the *Bishop of London,*
next to him the *Bishop of Durham,*
and then the *Bishop of Winchester.*
The others rank according to the
time of their *consecration,* that is, the
particular time they were first made
Bishops. They are all *Barons* and
Peers, and have a right of sitting in
the *House of Lords,* a place that will
be hereafter described. In order to
assist the Bishops there are persons
called

DEANS;

Who have under their direction
Clergymen, intitled

PREBENDARIES,

PREBENDARIES,

or

CANONS.

These are confulted when neceffary by the Bifhops, and when a Bifhop dies they are ordered by the King to elect another.

Next in the management of our church are Clergymen, called

ARCHDEACONS.

Whofe bufinefs is to reform abufes that may have crept into the church, and do any other things that the Bifhop may defire. Then come the

C   PARISH

PARISH PRIESTS,

or

RECTORS.

Their office is to do duty in the parifh churches, to fee that the *Pari-fhioners* (people that live in the parifh) attend public worfhip, to marry per-fons, to bury, to chriften children, and many other things. Laft of all are the

CURATES.

Thefe affift for certain falaries, the Rectors in the performance of their bufinefs.

There are other people though not Clergymen, who are employed about the church. The firft is the

CHURCH-

Church-Warden.

Whose office is to see that the church is in good repair, and that every thing is fit for divine worship. The next and last is the

Clerk;

Who is chosen by the parson. He is occasionally to read aloud in the church, and to give out and sing the psalms and hymns.

We now come to one of the most important parts of our government, namely,

The Parliament;

Which is a meeting composed of the first men in the nation. It consists of two parts, one called the

HOUSE

HOUSE OF LORDS, the other the HOUSE OF COMMONS. They are of great antiquity, and cannot open their first meeting without the King is present, or some other person to represent him. Their entire business is to consult and advise with one another on affairs of the nation. To make new laws, if necessary, and destroy of the old ones, those that are found to be of no use.

The parliament is summoned to meet in the following manner.

The King issues his writ, that is, his order to the *Lords Spiritual,* (the *Archbishops* and *Bishops* we before mentioned) and the *Lords Temporal* (meaning those Lords who do not belong to the Church) desiring them to appear at

a certain

a certain time and place, for the pur-
pose of giving their advice in certain
important affairs respecting the Church
and State, &c. A similar order is also
issued, directed to the Sheriff (a person
who will be explained hereafter) that
he may summon the people to choose
whom they please, to represent them
in the House of Commons. Those
who have the power of choosing, are
called *Electors*, and they must be *Free-
holders* (that is, possessors of freehold
land) to the value of forty shillings an-
nually, or else they have not any right
to interfere in the business.

Before a man can sit in parliament,
he must be of the age of twenty-one
years, and possess property in land to
a considerable amount. When in par-

C 3   liament

liament he cannot be arrested, that is,
his perfon cannot be taken for debt
as others may. Neither can his fer-
vants in conducting their mafter to
the Houfe of Commons, or from it,
be hindered in fo doing by any perfon
to whom they are indebted. Thefe are
called *privileges*, to which the members and their attendants are entitled.

The place where they generally,
and indeed always meet, is at *Weft-
minfter*, although the King, if he
choofes, may call them together in
whatever place he thinks proper. The
Lords fit in a room by themfelves,
and the Commons in another, which
was formerly a chapel called *St.
Stephen's*.

THE

THE MANNER OF SITTING IN THE
HOUSE OF LORDS.

The King whenever he comes (which
is now but at the opening of parliament, or the paffing of bills) is placed
at the upper end of the room in a very
grand chair, which is called a *chair
of ftate*, having a cloth of ftate over
his head. On his right hand is a feat
for the *Prince of Wales*, on his left
one for the *Duke of York*, the King's
fecond fon. Further on his right, on
a form, are the two *Archbifhops*, which
we mentioned before. Below thefe,
on another form, are the *Bifhops of
London*, *Durham*, and *Winchefter*.
Then upon other forms on the fame
fide, are all the other *Bifhops* placed
according to the time of their *confecra-
tion*,

tion, which, as we said before, means the particular time of their first being made Bishops. On the King's left hand upon forms are placed the *Lord Chancellor*, a man of great consequence in the state, and the head of a court which we shall hereafter describe. Also the King's *Treasurer*, *President of the King's Council*, and *Lord Privy Seal*, men of great learning, and whom the King consults on weighty affairs respecting the country. Others sit according to the time they first came to their titles; and in different parts of the house. There are various clerks and people appointed to do certain duties. One called *Gentleman Usher*, another a *Serjeant at Mace*, whose business is always to attend the *Chancellor*.

When

When the King is prefent, he always wears the crown upon his head, and none of the Lords are covered. When he is abfent the Lords at their entrance bow to the chair as if he was prefent.

THE MANNER OF THE MEMBERS SIT-TING IN THE HOUSE OF COMMONS.

The Members here fit promifcu-oufly, that is, without any order or ceremony. There is a perfon who has the conduct of the whole, called the *Speaker*. He is the only one who is fixed in a particular place in the Houfe. He fits in a large chair with clerks before him, and the Members to the right and left of him. They wear no robes as the Lords do, but whatever they think proper, such as they commonly appear in the ftreets

and

and among their friends. This is cer-
tainly unbecoming the dignity of fo
great a place, and ought to be reme-
died.

The time of their fitting is feldom
before four o'clock in the afternoon,
although the original intention was for
them to meet early in the morning.

When the time is come which was
fixed by the King's *writ*, or order, for
the parliament to affemble, the King
ufually appears in perfon in the Houfe
of Lords, with his crown on his head,
cloathed in the moft fuperb and ele-
gant robes. He then makes a fpeech,
telling them the caufe of his calling
them together, and the neceffity of their
doing fuch and fuch things, which he
mentions.

mentions. While he is speaking, the Lord Chancellor stands behind his chair, and the *Members of the House of Commons* at the same time bare at the bar. When the King has done, the Commons return to their own house, and choose from among themselves a person whom they call a *Speaker*, and whom we mentioned before. After he is appointed, each Member used to take the oath of *allegiance* (that is, proper obedience to the King) and also that of *supremacy*. This means that they will support this country against the power of the Pope, who was formerly considered supreme over all kingdoms, but which power, with respect to England, was thrown off by Henry VIII. Since that time it is usual for Members of the House of

Commons

Commons, and other perfons entering into profeffions, and into many public offices, to fwear that they acknowledge our fuperiority over the authority of the Pope. They now take new oaths appointed by an Act of Parliament paffed during the reign of William and Mary.

The powers, or as we faid before, the *privileges* of both Houfes of Parliament, are very great. They have not only the power of making laws, but putting a ftop to thofe that exift. This is called *repealing* them. The Lords have a right when they are fick, or when from any other caufe they cannot appear, to appoint others to act for them, who are called their *proxies.* So that it is thus fuppofed

that

that they are always prefent, doing their duty.

The Commons also have the power of making and repealing laws. For levying any money on the people (that is, compelling them to give fuch and fuch money for the ufe of the ftate) the bill begins in the Houfe of Commons, and not in the other houfe. This is called a *money bill*, and all that come under that title muft originate in the firft place, as the Members are fuppofed to be the people of England, who are alone to advance what fums that may be wanted. There are many other privileges which belong exclufively to the Houfe of Commons.

The

THE MANNER OF DEBATING AND
PASSING BILLS.

A Bill is a kind of an Addrefs, pointing out the neceffity of enacting (that
is, making) fome new law. This may
be propofed by any one of the Members, either in the *Houfe of Lords* or
Houfe of Commons. If in the latter it
is prefented by the Speaker, and when
read, it is either at once rejected or
elfe allowed to be debated, and a
certain time appointed for the fecond
reading, after which it muft be rejected, or ordered to be confidered
by a certain number of the Houfe,
called a *Committee.* After they have
confidered and amended it, and twice
read it two different days, then it is *en-*
groffed, that is, written fair on *parch-*
                                    ment,

ment, and afterwards read a third time. The Speaker then demands whether it fhall pafs into a law or not, when the *majority* (that is, the greater number of the Members) determines.

At the time a Bill is fent by the Commons up to the Lords, it is ufual for feveral Members to attend. When they come up to the bar of the Houfe of Lords, the Member who has it, makes three bows, and delivers it to the Lord Chancellor, who comes down from his feat for that purpofe.

An almoft fimilar ceremony is ufed when a Bill is fent from the Lords to the Commons.

When

When any one in the House of Commons wifhes to fpeak on a Bill, he ftands up uncovered, and directs his fpeech only to the Speaker. If what he fays be completely anfwered by another, he is not allowed to fpeak again on the fame bufinefs that day, to prevent the whole time being taken up by the converfation of two people. This is not attended to when the whole Houfe is formed into a *Committee* (which we explained before) for then every Member may fpeak as often as he thinks proper.

If in either Houfe any one fpeaks improper words, he is called to the bar, where he is fometimes compelled to go down on his knees, and in that fituation receives a reprimand from

from the Speaker. If the offence be very great, then he is sent to the *Tower*.

The Members give their assent or diſſent to the paſſing of a Bill, by ſaying, *yea*, or *no*. The firſt pronounced aloud by all thoſe who wiſh it to paſs, the laſt by thoſe who do not. When it is doubtful which is the greater number, then the Houſe *divides*, that is, one ſet or the other go out, that each may be reckoned.

The Lords in the other Houſe give their votes by ſaying, *content* or *not content*.

If a Bill paſs both the *Houſe of Commons* and *Houſe of Lords*, then it

is

is brought up with others that have also paſſed the two houſes, to the King, who comes again to the Lords with his crown on his head, dreſſed in his robes as before, and being ſeated in the ſame chair of ſtate in which he firſt opened the parliament, the clerk reads the title of each Bill, and another clerk by the deſire of the King, pronounces his Majeſty's aſſent or diſſent, one by one as they are read.

Sometimes this is done when the King is not preſent, by another empowered by his Majeſty to act for him.

When all thoſe things for which the parliament was ſummoned, have been gone through and finiſhed, then the

the King adjourns, prorogues, or dis-
solves it.

The first means that the house
should suspend their meetings to some
other day. The second, that they
should end the session entirely for that
year; and the third, that the parliament should be *dissolved*, that is, broke
up, and that a new one should be
again formed in the same manner we
before described. The parliament has
a right to adjourn itself, but when it
is *prorogued* or *dissolved*, then his Ma-
jesty most commonly does it in person.

After having fully and clearly explained that most important part of
the English government, called the
Parliament,

Parliament, we shall now give the reader a description of our courts of justice, and the first that offers itself is the

KING'S BENCH.

This court is called the King's Bench, becaufe in former times the Kings ufed frequently to fit there. It is there that the King may try his fubjects for any crime againft the ftate or himfelf, or any private difpute refpecting the payment of money between one perfon and another, may alfo be tried there, and its power is very confiderable.

In this court four judges are appointed to fit for the difpatch of bufinefs. The firft is ftiled *Lord Chief*

Juftice

Juſtice of the King's Bench, and his place is given to him by his Majeſty. The reſt are alſo appointed by him, and hold their places by *Letters Patent,* that is, they cannot be taken away from them. Theſe judges have regular yearly ſalaries paid to them by the King.

All young gentlemen, when they are called to the bar, are allowed to practiſe in this court, the power, or what is ſometimes called *juriſdiction,* of which extends all over England.

The Court of Chancery.

This court is called a Court of Equity, becauſe in its determinations, *equity* and *good conſcience* are blended

with

with the rules of law. It is intended to check, or what is termed, to *mitigate* the severity of our other courts.

THE LORD CHANCELLOR,

Is the only judge of this court. He holds the higheſt office of any in England under his Majeſty.

MASTERS OF CHANCERY.

The Chancellor has twelve aſſiſt-ants that are ſo called. The firſt of theſe is the

MASTER OF THE ROLLS.

This is a place of great dignity, and is in the gift of the King during his pleaſure.

The

The Court of Chancery is always open for the performance of bufinefs, when the other courts only fit at certain ftated times in the year, called *Term Time.* So that any perfon oppreffed at whatever period, may have redrefs in this court, although the others may be clofed.

The next court for the execution of the laws is the

COURT OF COMMON PLEAS.

So called, in confequence of formerly this court alone being intended for deciding any matter or plea between fubject and fubject.

The chief juftice in this court, is called *Lord Chief Juftice of the Common Pleas,*

Pleas, or *Common Bench.* He holds his place by *Letters Patent,* which we before described, and so do the other inferior judges, of which there are three.

Caufes between one man and another are tried here, and so they are in the Court of King's Bench, but those in which the King is concerned are never tried in the first court, but most generally in the latter.

Those that plead or do business in the Common Pleas, are what are called *Serjeants at Law,* and none else can.

There are many clerks and officers belong to this court.

The

The next and laſt is the

COURT OF EXCHEQUER.

Here are tried all cauſes that reſpect the King's *Treaſury*, in which
the money that enables the government to proceed with the buſineſs of
the nation is kept, and any account
that in the leaſt concerns him. This
court was at firſt confined to this kind
of buſineſs, but of late years, any
perſon may proceed in it for the re-
covery of any debt that may be owing
to him, as in the other courts.

In the Exchequer are *ſix judges*, the
chief of which is called

E   CHANCELLOR

CHANCELLOR OF THE EXCHEQUER.

But he never appears in the court, having other matters of great confequence to attend to. The others all do, the firft of whom is ftiled

LORD CHIEF BARON.

His office is alfo held by *Patent*, and the other judges are all called *Barons of the Exchequer.*

Having now given a brief account of the government of all England in general, we fhall next defcribe the particular GOVERNMENT of COUNTIES, CITIES, BOROUGHS, and VILLAGES.

JUSTICES

JUSTICES OF THE PEACE.

For the management of each county, the King appoints a person of considerable consequence, an inhabitant of the place, to preserve the peace and good order of the county. He is called *Justice of the Peace*, and his duty is to call before him, examine and commit to prison all thieves, rogues, vagabonds, and all others that occasion a breach of the peace, and there to remain until they are brought up to the

QUARTER SESSIONS.

These are meetings every three months at some principal town in the county; composed of the several justices

tices of the adjoining counties. Upon
examination, if it be thought that any
of the prisoners are guilty of *treaſon*,
murder, or any other capital offence,
then they are immediately committed
to priſon, in order to take their trial at
the next *Aſſizes* (particular times in
the year when the judges belonging
to the courts at Weſtminſter come
down to the country for the purpoſe
of trying the priſoners.) For the more
eaſy and better execution of the laws,
the King once a year nominates, or
appoints for each county, a perſon
called

A SHERIFF.

Whoſe duty it is, among other
things, to execute whatever orders
the King tranſmits to him, to attend
to

to all *writs* directed to him, that iſſue
or come from the courts at Weſtminſter, and to accompany all thoſe
unfortunate people who are ſentenced
to death; for it is the Sheriff's buſineſs to ſee it done, in which he is
aſſiſted by the *under Sheriff*, *Clerks*,
Bailiffs, *Conſtables*, and *Gaolers*, all under his command.

There are ſeveral other places of
truſt in each county, in order to perform the neceſſary buſineſs.

Of the Government of Cities, Boroughs, and Villages.

Every city in England is governed
like a little kingdom of itſelf. The
inhabitants chooſe from among them-
ſelves twelve perſons whom they call

Aldermen,

Alderman, and one of these is appointed head over the others, and he bears the name of *Mayor.* He is considered a kind of judge over the whole place, and he has a power of trying, in his own court, almost every offence, but the cause may be moved by the parties to any of the higher courts at Westminster.

BOROUGHS.

These are nothing more than large villages with such and such privileges granted to them by the King, and they are thus called *incorporated.* In that case they are governed pretty nearly in the same manner as the cities and towns.

VILLAGES.

VILLAGES.

In thefe are appointed perfons called *Petty Conftables*, chofen every year for the purpofe of keeping the peace, and fecuring all thofe that are riotous, or fufpected of being offenders, and bringing them before the next Juftice, under whofe controul they are.

OF THE LAWS OF ENGLAND.

OF THE COMMON LAW.

The Common Law of England means the common cuftoms of the kingdom that have by length of time obtained the force of laws.

Befides the common law, there are in various parts of England cuftoms

toms and common practices which have the force of common law, among thofe people to whofe property they belong.

STATUTE LAW.

Where the common law is filent, then comes in the *Statute Law*. This is made by the King, by and with the advice of his parliament.

All trials of common and ftatute law are by *twelve men*, called a *jury*. Thefe are fummoned by the fheriff to meet, and while the lawyers are pleading on both fides in open court before the judges, thefe twelve men ftand by, and hear all that is faid and produced on either part, and may afk

what

what queftions they pleafe of the witneffes. When all the witneffes are ex-
amined, one of the judges briefly ftates
all that has paft, pointing out to them
thofe parts that are according to law,
and what are not, after which they re-
tire by themfelves, and until they all
agree upon the bufinefs, they are not
allowed to have any meat, drink, fire,
nor candle. When they are agreed
they come back into court, and the
foreman, who is fo called from his
being placed firft on the lift of the
twelve jurymen, declares the opi-
nion of all the jury, for every one
of them muft agree, and the fentence
thus finally paffes.

CIVIL

CIVIL LAW.

When the *Common* and *Statute Law* takes no notice, then comes in the *Civil Law*. This is made ufe of in all courts refpecting the church, which are called *Ecclefiaftical Courts*. In every thing refpecting wills of people deceafed, fometimes called *Teftaments*, the civil law is refered to, alfo in all things where the church is concerned, and in affairs immediately relating to the King's fleets and other veffels.

BY-LAWS.

By the King's permiffion, or what is more generally called by his *Royal Charter*, granted to various cities in England, the magiftrates have a power

to

to make fuch laws, as may be thought of fervice to the inhabitants, but, at the fame time, they muft not go to op-pofe the laws of the land, and they have no force but in the particular place they are made.

FOREST LAWS.

The *Foreft Laws* are peculiar laws, and differ from the common law of England. Our forefts in this coun-try are exceedingly ancient, and, in former times, offences committed in any of them were punifhed by the King in the moft fevere manner. But in thefe days punifhments are more lenient for offences committed in any of the King's forefts, and they all come under the correction of the *Foreft Laws.* MARTIAL

MARTIAL LAW.

This means that law which depends
upon the King's will and pleasure in
time of war, during which, in some
particular alarming cases of danger,
he orders out the military, and when
martial law is proclaimed, the country
is then under the government of the
soldiers. This is never done but in
the greatest necessity.

OF THOSE LAWS RESPECTING WOMEN.

Respecting the women of England,
there are many things of considerable
consequence in our laws and customs.
Women in this country, with all their
property, so soon as they are married,
are wholly at the will and disposal of
the husband.   If

If any goods or property of any kind are given to a married woman, they immediately become her huf- band's, and fhe cannot part with them or fell them without his confent.

The wife can make no contract, that is, agreement, without her hufband's confent.

The law of England fuppofes the power the hufband has over his wife, is as great as over his child, and there- fore he muft anfwer for his wife's faults. If fhe wrong another with her tongue, or in any other way, he muft make fatisfaction.

So the law makes it as high a crime, and allots the fame punifhment to a woman who kills her hufband, as to a

F   woman

woman who kills her father or mother, and it is called *petit-treafon.*

The woman upon marriage lofes not only the power over her property, but alfo her name—for ever after fhe ufes her hufband's firname, and her own is wholly laid afide, which is not the cafe in many other countries.

The wife, after her hufband's death, having nothing fettled on her before marriage, which is called her *jointure,* may lawfully lay claim to a *third part* of his yearly rents of land during her life, and within the City of London may take a *third part* of all her hufband's property in money, goods, and all property except land, and which is called *perfonal property.*

As

As the wife takes her hufband's name, fo likewife does fhe partake of his condition. If he be a *Duke*, fhe is called a *Duchefs*, and if he be a *Knight*, fhe is called a *Lady*.

By the laws of England, married perfons are fo faft joined that they cannot be wholly parted by any agreement between themfelves, but only by fentence of the judges. The wife is confidered fo much the fame with her hufband, that fhe cannot be produced as a witnefs for or againft him.

OF CHILDREN.

The condition of children in England is very different from that in other countries.

F 3   As

As hufbands have more abfolute authority over their wives, fo fathers have a greater authority over their children.

Fathers may give, if they pleafe, all their property to one child alone, and none to the reft. This confideration ought to keep children obedient to their fathers.

By the *common law* (which was before explained) in England, children at certain ages are enabled to perform certain acts.

A fon, at the age of fourteen, may by will difpofe of goods and all his property, excepting lands, which he cannot take poffeffion of until he arrives at the age of twenty-one.

At

At the age of fifteen, he may be sworn to his *allegiance* to the King, that is, to be true and faithful to him.

At twenty-one, he is said to be at full age, may then do as he thinks proper with either his goods, money, which is called *personal property*, or his lands, which is called *real property*.

OF SERVANTS.

The present condition of servants in England is much more comfortable than it was in former times. They were then confidered very little better than flaves, but now they have the power of appealing to the laws of their country for redress, in case of their being injured.

A servant

A servant to take away the life of a master is considered a very high crime, and is called *petit-treason*, and is punished with death.

There are no slaves permitted to live in England. A foreign slave brought over into this country, is, upon his landing, immediately free from slavery, and enjoys the same protection of the laws equally with us all.

OF THE PUNISHMENTS INFLICTED IN ENGLAND.

All crimes in England that reach the life of a man are either *High-treason, Petty-treason, Rape, Murder, Felony,* together with some others.

Some

Some high treasons are much more heinous and odious than others, yet the same punishment is inflicted by the law for them all.

A person guilty of this crime, suffers death. All his lands and goods whatsoever are forfeited. His wife shall lose some of her rights, and his children all their right of inheriting from him, or any other of his ancestors.

Coining of money is considered *high-treason*, and consequently punished with death.

Petty-treason, which is when a servant kills his master or mistress, or a wife kills her husband, is punished with death.   *Felony,*

Felony, which is next in degree to *petit-treason*, is punished with death. There are some felonies however, in which the criminal is only marked with a red hot iron on the hand.

Great Larceny is when the goods stolen exceed the value of *one shilling*, and the punishment is death.

Petty Larceny is when the goods stolen is under the value of one shilling, and the punishment is generally whipping, or some other punishment inflicted on the person.

Perjury, swearing what is not true, is punished in general with the pillory.

Forgery,

Forgery, which is forging, or imitating the name of another person, is a very great offence, and almost always punished with death.

For striking any person in any of the King's Courts, whereby blood is spilt, the punishment is, that the criminal shall have his right hand cut off.

When any person kills himself, it is called *Felo de se*, and the body is interred without the usual burial service repeated, as is done to all christians. There is also a stake driven through the corpse.

INNS

INNS OF COURT.

These are places wherein the Students study the laws of the kingdom, to render them capable of practising in the courts of law at Westminster, which we have before particularly mentioned. They are four in number, namely, the

INNER TEMPLE,

MIDDLE TEMPLE,

LINCOLN'S INN,

and

GRAY'S INN.

The other Inns are these.

THE TWO SERJEANTS' INNS,

and eight Inns of Chancery,

called

CLIFFORD'S

CLIFFORD'S INN,
SYMOND'S INN,
CLEMENT'S INN,
NEW INN,
LYON'S INN,
FURNIVAL'S INN,
STAPLE'S INN,
BERNARD'S INN,
and
THAVIE'S INN.

The Inns of Courts are governed by what are called *Mafters, Principals, Benchers, Stewards,* and other Officers, and have public Halls for Exercifes, Readings, and Argument. Thefe the Students muft attend for a certain number of years before they can be admitted to plead at the Bar.

We

We now bring our little volume to a conclufion, trufting that we have faithfully performed during our progrefs what we promifed at our firft fetting out, namely, to treat the feveral fubjects intended to be explained, in fuch a plain and fimple manner, as to make them perfectly eafy to be underftood by thofe youths who are to be brought up to the profeffion. In doing this, we flatter ourfelves we fhall be of no inconfiderable fervice to them, as our labours are intended principally to clear the way for a more extenfive inveftigation of the different matters herein contained, and thereby be the means of rendering the perufal of *Blackftone's Commentaries*, more beneficial to the youthful Reader than formerly.

F I N I S

www.ingramcontent.com/pod-product-compliance
Lightning Source LLC
Chambersburg PA
CBHW081723270326
41933CB00017B/3272